Paleo Diet Cookbook for Beginners

Lose Weight and Feel Great with These Easy to Prepare Paleo Diet Recipes

Elisa Williams

TABLE OF CONTENTS

Introduction to Paleo Diet

A paleo diet food list is that the ideal diet that depends on the dietary requirements set up all through the transformative way to the current sort for the human creatures - having the natural name of Homo sapiens. Paleo diet is moreover known as the naturally worthy diet. The stylish dietary routine is alluded to as the Paleo diet food list shortened as a Paleo diet or paleo diet, which is also prominently called the caveman diet, tracker assembled diet, or Stone Age diet. Paleo food of that period comprised wild plants and wild creatures devoured by the men of the said time. Paleolithic age finished with the advancement of ongoing horticultural procedures and thoughts around 10,000 years prior. The subject behind the idea about the practicality of the Paleolithic diet for humans is that the legitimate diet for human well-being ought to be intently like the genealogical diet. A Paleo diet food rundown ought to be made out of them on top of referenced fixings. Starting with the meat, that ought to be eaten as a ton of joined will however the reason to recall is that the meat should be cooked basic without adding a great deal of the fats because fats cause a few infections like pulse, cholesterol and increment the odds of deadly respiratory failure by obstructing the section of blood flow. By remembering this time, meat is solid for us whether we use it inside the morning meal, lunch, or supper. Lean beef is the beef managed of noticeable fats, and the lean meats rundown can be extended to contain the lean hamburger, flank steak, extra-lean burger, lean veal, Chunk steak, London cooks, Top sirloin steak, and any unique slim cut. Lean poultry comprises chicken bosom, turkey bosom, and game hen bosom having chicken with skin eliminated. Eggs at most extreme six in seven days of duck, goose, and chicken (select the enhanced Omega 3 choice of chicken eggs).

Elective sorts of meat may fuse bunny and goat meat. Game meat should comprise crocodile, bear, buffalo or bison, kangaroo, and so forth. Fish meat is likewise ideal to be utilized as a diet. The meat inside the Paleo diet food list comes to the number of products of the soil vegetables. A few people believe that products of the soil increment the weight and make them fat. Comparable to the higher than, this can be unmistakably the main misguided judgment regarding the incorporation of organic products inside the way of life. Natural products don't expand the load at all, paying little mind to how bountiful you eat it as leafy foods vegetables contains extremely low measures of calories. For the ideal life and well-being, every dinner should exemplify a mix of meat, salad, vegetables, nuts, seeds, and natural products like apples, pomegranates, grapes, apricots, figs, and bananas in his diet. Oranges, lemon, pears, pineapples, watermelons, and Papaya are among the renowned natural products because they contain higher water measure and subsequently give additional energy to the benefactor. As to different foodstuffs remembered for the Paleo diet, in an episode of effectively getting more fit, at the most extreme, four ounces of nuts and seeds ought to be utilized. Pecans are among the easiest because they contain the most significant proportion of Omega 3. Oils, drinks, and Paleo desserts should conjointly be utilized in moderate amounts. Furthermore, recollect that Paleo diet food rundown won't contain everything handled foods made out of a dairy item, powdered milk, frozen yogurts, oat grains, and vegetables and should be kept away from. The overall low-carb diets shun eating any carbs while the Paleo Diet nuts and bolts epitomize things like new foods grown from the ground.

The Paleo Diet also doesn't accept any dairy that might be a major dietary disadvantage for a few groups. Such a large number of long stretches of chemical-bound milk has made even people who should endure dairy well touchy or even oversensitive to it. The Paleo Diet incredibly centers around more modest pieces of upper-quality supplements by definition. The Paleo diet, likewise called the Paleolithic Diet, could be a dietary arrangement that is predicated on the assumed diet of our progenitors living inside the Paleolithic period. Such cases are as yet discussed these days by specialists and well-being experts. Indeed, even consequently, since the renewed introduction of this diet mastermind, it has been considered by a few in show effective arrangement accomplish a better life. The prior arrangement of the Paleo diet plan is to burn through foods that are eatable in their normal state or the event that it does might want to be cooked. It should be, at any rate, set up in the best methods feasible. It is designed by the way of life of our predecessors who survived demonstrations of looking, fishing, and assembling edible plants. The accommodation of cooking wasn't out there around then.

I amazingly like concerning this diet because I just

fundamentally need to bring up a practical issue after thinking about a portion of certain food. If I was living in the Stone age, would this food be offered to me? It's eye-catching to consider that while the people of that day neglected to have the innovation or the indistinguishable abundance of food that we tend to savor these days, that they, in a real sense, we're in a situation to deliver their bodies with more characteristic foods and supplements in each meat that they ate. People searching for a good dieting plan might be overpowered by the number of choices for dinner designs out there. The Paleo diet or caveman diet takes its motivation from the human tribal air itself, at least reliable with our speculations worried that point sum. People in the familial setting didn't eat stylishly prepared foods. Anyway, they might not have eaten any of the foods that we will, in general, presently accompany an agricultural way of life. Dairy products, bread, and grain stock are farming in nature. This diet is tied in with returning to our underlying foundations to an enormous degree, subsequently to talk. This diet fuses various distinctive dietary standards. There has been a generous amount of discussion over the years on whether individuals should lessen their admission of fats or starches. The contention gets even extra confounded when people bring up whether it's a straightforward matter of practicing good eating habits, fats, and sound cards and keeping away from their undesirable partners. Paleo comes out rigorously on the discussion that favors fats over sugars. However, it will, in general, accentuate monounsaturated fats instead of immersed fats.

The Paleo diet puts an exacting weight on eating the lean cuts of meat. In general, this diet is low in sugars. People eating the ordinary Western diet will get the vast majority of their sugars from bread and improved drinks. On the Paleo diet, the vast majority of your carbs can return from leafy foods, which are normally low in calories and accordingly contain relatively a couple of carbs. In a nutshell, people on the Paleo will burn through meat, natural products, vegetables, and nuts, oils, and flavors. Dairy items and grain items are off the menu. There is a significant measure of a continuous conversation concerning the general advantages of the Paleo diet. Anyway, some qualities will well advance well-being by their own doing. For a certain something, individuals can understand themselves devouring not very many undesirable prepared foods while on the Paleo diet, and handled foods can be loaded down with unfortunate and untested food added substances. A few nutritionists and dieticians concur that refined sugar is unfortunate, and individuals will acknowledge eating pretty much zero teaspoons of refined sugar while on this diet. While numerous other low-starch diets tend to be too high in unfortunate fats, the Paleo places an exceptional weight on nuts and seeds' fats, which numerous dieticians and nutritionists recommend modestly.

Though the basic study of the Paleo diet is continually under examination, a few of its key standards appear to be founded on sound dietary hypothesis. A few groups beginning Paleo could see it depleting to deal with at first. For certain people, it may address a stunning dietary change. People may wind up cooking extra regularly to get ready delicious Paleo recipes. The developing prevalence of the Paleo diet should help make progress simpler for people curious about improving their well-being. Regularly known as the caveman diet because of its reference to being a Stone Age diet, the Paleo Diet is nothing extra than eating foods that are, for the most part, common. For instance, the sorts of foods that are considered satisfactory in this diet can be individuals who might be out there all through the Stone Age time. It would comprise wild plants, nuts, vegetables, meat, fish, and whatever foods devoured in their normal state. Essentially, this diet will comprise foods that might be eaten normally or prepared in a very way that is extremely basic, when every one of our precursors didn't have electric ovens, microwaves, or elective popular gadgets to arrange their food. Thus, this diet is designed according to that kind of way of life. You won't wander out chasing your food, choosing your vegetables, or running from wild creatures. Anyway, you'll make essential picks of foods that are generally regular and entirety. It expects that we tend to are organically fit to eating the way these antiquated progenitors of our own did. They ate the foods that were promptly accessible, high in healthful worth, contemporary, and indeed, bereft of added substances or preparing.

The foods they ate were high in protein, low in fat, awful fats, and contained all the fiber, nutrients, and minerals a sound body needs. Though simultaneously wiping out the terrible fats, sugars, and void calories (seared foods, candy, liquor, and refined grains) that have caused us, as a country, to be overweight and ridden with constant infection. The Paleo diet evades many of the foods we grew up reasoning about a fundamental piece of a sound diet - foods like grains (bread, oats, wafers, tortillas, and pasta) and dairy items (milk, cheeses, yogurt, frozen yogurt). In any case, these are the foods that can bring about the chief weight acquire - they contain undeniable degrees of carbs, fats, and salt. Eating them in enormous amounts contributes not exclusively to acquire yet to other well-being dangers, for example, diabetes and hypertension. Numerous competitors have accepted the Paleo diet due to its weight on protein from lean meats, fish, and poultry. Adding the new vegetables and natural products adds extra protein and a wide range of various fundamental nutrients, minerals, and fiber. The fresher and greener the vegetables, the better. Green, verdant vegetables like broccoli, spinach, kale, and different greens contain fundamental minerals like potassium and magnesium that few Americans lack in their diets. Furthermore, on the off chance that you'll have the option to get natural vegetables, that is far superior. The Paleo diet incorporates foods that can be pursued or accumulated, very much as they have been for an extremely prolonged period.

Fish and meats will be pursued, for example, and mushrooms, seeds, vegetables, and eggs can be assembled. The diet bars foods and added substances that didn't appear to be in the primary human diet. It incorporates grains, vegetables, prepared oils, and dairy items. Maybe the chief unfamiliar substance in the vogue human diet is recommended drugs. Paleo will, in general, devour drugs in crises and, in any case, dispose of them from their regular diet. Paleo expects to imitate the conventional way of life from multiple perspectives than simply the diet, albeit the diet is the chief fundamental way. They walk shoeless to create more grounded feet; give their bodies masses of time to rest during both evening and day; pay stacks of time outside - anything they can expect of that will adjust their ways of life to that of an ancient caveman.

Benefits of Paleo Diet

The paleo diet can be characterized as a healthy diet that exclusively permits the utilization of characteristic foods like meat, vegetables, and solid fats like coconut oils, macadamia oils, olive oils, etc. It restricts the utilization of grains, grain-basically based food items, sugar, and any very handled food. Characteristic all the way. That is the way into the paleo diet. Style might want not to be forfeited. Flavors might be utilized, and there are a few magnificent paleo formula books accessible that will instruct you to prepare sound, anyway delectable dishes. The underlying benefit to the paleo diet can be a decreased danger of infection.

Most people are utilized to the current diet with additives, destructive added substances, and diverse fake fixings that cause a wide range of medical problems and weight. Changing to the paleo diet will kill a large portion of these issues. The subsequent benefit can be a deficiency of abundance fat. The paleo diet means to downsize the number of carbs you devour. It can keep your glucose levels stable and increment your insulin affectability. That recommends that your body will be extra fixed on consuming off fat and remaining fit. The decrease of irritation is the third advantage. A large number of people, wherever the planet, grumbles of everyday a throbbing painfulness. Their body harms, yet they are doing not handle why. The explanation is aggravation because of the utilization of undesirable foods. The cells are aroused from the food they ate. By changing to the paleo diet, you might be devouring an extremely solid diet. It will lessen all aggravation and increment your feeling of prosperity. The fourth benefit is expanded bulk. Since the paleo diet spins around the utilization of bountiful meat measures, you will get a pile of protein. It will help in muscle development and recovery if you communicate in standard exercise. There will be bountiful less muscle breakdown. A great deal of muscle you have, the extra calories you consume. It essentially implies that you'll be lean, match, and solid. A better mind and organs are the fifth benefit.

The 6th advantage is decreased propensity to encourage sensitivities. Stylish day foods contain fixings that raise people's affectability to allergens. By removing these foods, our capacity to encourage hypersensitivities is enormously decreased. The seventh benefit is expanded energy. At first, the diet might be almost no intense to follow, and you'll not feel savvy because your body is freeing itself from poisons gathered from past dietary patterns. The change in diet additionally will be troublesome. However, when you live through this mound, it very well may be smooth cruising all the methodology. You'll understand yourself loaded with life and overflowing with energy. The higher than seven reasons should be sufficient to direct you to give up the paleo diet an attempt. You won't ever think back, and most people on the paleo diet say that it is one in every one of the least difficult things they could do. The way that the Paleo framework remains getting utilized today ought to demonstrate how successful it's.

By separating a person's admission to the principal fundamental, Paleo devotees figure out how to eliminate the modern sugars that litter popular food and because weight acquire. Henceforth, it just is reasonable that they will begin to get thinner - even with not many exercise meetings. Indeed, exercises for Paleo supporters are generally confined to a short however incredible burst that will rapidly consume off energy without drawing out the distress. With everything taken into account, the Paleo diet is an unimaginably successful philosophy of getting thinner. Be that as it may, one in everything about high issues of people utilizing Paleo is the absence of flavor and determination in their food. As referenced, some books give tips and deceive to Paleo experts to cook tasty dishes while not wandering from the Paleo idea. Henceforth, individuals who need to endeavor out this weight reduction routine don't have anything frozen. This diet is low in sugar and sodium because an excess of salt in the body isn't solid. Stone age men didn't have a stack of sugar or sodium in their diet because fake sugars, sugar, and salt didn't exist the way they will today. There was no requirement for unnecessary added substances. It was all unsettling enduring. The Paleo diet is tied in with returning to the basics by eating meat, contemporary organic product, contemporary vegetables, and staying away from a wide range of prepared foods that weren't accessible inside the Paleolithic period. In case you're attempting to get thinner, this is frequently the diet for you. It can work with your thin down because you might be eating enough of the legitimate things that your body will handle on what to attempt to with it and how to appropriately technique it. In flip, you'll practice which can urge your body to utilize your protein to assemble muscle, consume fat and eventually get more fit. In contrast to different diets, you'll have the option to get joy from your food by browsing recipes imprinted in an incredibly paleo formula book.

Paleo formula books embrace an assortment of heavenly dishes, similar to breakfast dinners of omelet biscuits, wiener pan-fried food, and steak and eggs. There isn't any need to skip dinners as the paleo diet needs you to eat when you are ravenous. This way, snacks like paleo hummus, an unpracticed smoothie, and bacon-wrapped dates can be made in your kitchen. Some paleo formula books conjointly incorporate soups like buffalo stew, gazpacho, and paleo meat stew for a luxurious dinner. Furthermore, elective paleo formula books embrace a shift of substantial dishes that cowl hamburger, poultry, and other game meats. You decidedly won't feel like you are on a tight eating routine as you chew into pork cook with a Dijon coat or have a couple of bun-less burgers in the middle of breaks at work. Sides like paleo pesto, simmered asparagus, basil spinach, and broccoli supplement these huge protein dishes.

While well-being edges of the paleo diet to get more fit are a motivating force to bear this severe diet, the well-being benefits are empowering. Alongside weight reduction, these common foods are perceived to help settle circulatory strain and cholesterol to solid levels while expanding energy, an undertaking the body can't do when over-burden with handled foods and sugar. The unmistakable medical advantages of this particular diet are a more grounded resistant safeguard in warding off sickness and infection, subsequently wiping out numerous well-being chances that are hence broad nowadays. For regardless of reason, you decide to be on a tight eating routine that began millennia prior. The characteristic foods alone can have a crucial enhancement for your well-being and essentialness. Seeds, nuts, natural products, vegetables, eggs, fish, and meat are regular Paleo diet foods. Low-quality nourishments like cakes, confections, sugars and baked goods are excluded from this diet, just like a genuine clarification for metabolic condition. Handled foods, dairy products, grains, and vegetable oils are prohibited from this diet. Even though meat might be a significant portion of the Paleo diet, foods like bacon, pepperoni, pork hotdogs, chicken wings, and store item should be kept away from the following fat substance. Grain and wheat items, including oats, rice, and grain, ought to be kept away from totally.

Foods grown from the ground are a fundamental piece

of this diet. They make for a solid nibble in the middle of suppers, regarding the foods devoured by stone-age men, all horticultural items, just as gluten-free ones, are excluded during this diet. One of the principal advantages of this diet is that processing will balance out at last. It expands digestion, promoting weight reduction. Since the Paleo diet has high protein content, a ton of competitors follow this diet. The fundamental foods like fish, chicken, nuts and slender meat give fiber and energy to the competitors promoting muscle advancement and weight decrease. Casein and gluten are the main sources of hypersensitivities, and they are found in a few prepared foods. In any case, they are not a portion of the Paleo diet foods, and thus, any can use this diet without worrying about stricken by hypersensitive responses. The danger of getting weight-associated sicknesses like diabetes and heart infections is impressively brought down since the Paleo diet consolidates a high fiber and low starch content. This magnificent diet setup incredibly profits a huge load of people.

Gluten-Free Paleo Tomato Scrambled Eggs

Preparation Time: 35 Minutes

Cooking Time: 10 Minutes

Servings: 3

Ingredients:

- Half tsp. dried parsley
- One-fourth mug (30 gram) cheese, ground
- Four eggs
- One-fourth mug (60 milliliters) rice milk
- Half mug (27 gram) sun-dried tomatoes

Instructions:

- If using dried tomatoes, boil water in a pot. Switch off the heat and put tomatoes in water for about five minutes until soft. Chop up tomatoes in small pieces.
- Whisk together eggs and milk. Put egg batter in greased dish. Add tomato pieces, cheddar cheese, and parsley. Scramble until done.

Nutritional Analysis:

Calories: 232, Fat: 11g, Carbohydrates: 19g, Sodium: 47mg, Protein: 2g, Net carbs: 3g

Low-Fat Asian Egg Fry

Preparation Time: 35 Minutes

Cooking Time: 15 Minutes

Servings: 3

Ingredients:

- one tsp. baking grains
- four oz. (115 gram) canned chilies, chopped
- two mugs (450 gram) cottage cheddar cheese
- Half mug (half a gram) without salt butter
- ten eggs
- Half mug (63 gram) flour

Instructions:

- Whisk eggs; add flour and baking grains. Add butter and then add chilies, cottage cheddar cheese, and Monterey Jack. Add into a saucepan.
- Prepare at 400-degree Fahrenheit for 15 minutes. Decrease the heat to 250-degree Fahrenheit and prepare a further 315 minutes.

Low Carb Low-Fat Mixed Fruit Smoothie

Preparation Time: 20 Minutes

Cooking Time: 10 Minutes

Servings: 2

Ingredients:

- two mugs (460 gram) small-fat peach yogurt
- one mug (145 gram) blueberries
- two mugs (300 gram) diced banana

Instructions:

- Merge all ingredients in a blender and then serve right away immediately with honey and mint.

Snowy Day Breakfast Casserole

Preparation Time: 45 Minutes

Cooking Time: 15 Minutes

Servings: 2

Ingredients:

- One-fourth mug (37 gram) green bell pepper, chopped
- four eggs
- One-fourth mug (30 gram) small fat Cheddar cheese, ground
- two slices of small bacon
- three potatoes, ground
- Half mug (80 gram) onion, chopped

Instructions:

- Preheat the oven to 350 degrees F. In a large dish, prepare the bacon. Shift the bacon on a paper towel–covered pan. In a pan, prepare the potatoes, onion, and green pepper until the potatoes are crispy and the onion is tender.
- In a mixing bowl, blend the crumbled bacon and the mayonnaise. Transfer to an eight-inch (20-

centimeter) square baking plate that has been greased. Pour the eggs on top. Serve with a sprinkling of cheddar cheese—Cook for about 15 minutes or until the eggs are complete.

Vegetable Fry Egg

Preparation Time: 30 Minutes

Cooking Time: 10 Minutes

Servings: 3

Ingredients:

- One-fourth mug (37 gram) green bell peppers, diced
- One-fourth mug (28 gram) zucchini, diced
- Half mug (90 gram) tomato, diced
- one tbsp. (15 milliliters) olive oil
- two oz. (55 gram) mushrooms, diced
- One-fourth mug (40 gram) onion, diced
- four eggs
- , two tbsp. (30 gram) fat-free sour cream
- two tbsp. (30 milliliters) water
- two oz. (55 gram) Swiss cheddar cheese, ground

Instructions:

- Add olive oil to a big dish and fry mushrooms, onion, green bell pepper, zucchini, and tomato until soft, adding tomato last.
- Whisk together eggs, sour cream, and water until fluffy. Cover an omelet saucepan or dish with nonstick vegetable spray and put over moderate-high heat. Add egg batter into a saucepan.
- Lift the edges as it cooks to allow uncooked egg to run underneath. When eggs are nearly set, cover half the eggs with the cheddar cheese and fried vegetables and fold the other half. Continue preparing until eggs are completely set.

Nutritional Analysis:

Calories: 245, Fat: 14g, Carbohydrates: 10g, Sodium: 18mg, Protein: 2g, Net carbs: 3g

Breakfast Enchiladas

Preparation Time: 60 Minutes

Cooking Time: 30 Minutes

Servings: 2

Ingredients:

- two Half mugs (300 gram) minced Cheddar cheese
- eight whole wheat tortillas
- four eggs
- two mugs (475 milliliters), rice milk
- one tbsp. flour
- 12 oz. (340 gram) ham, finely chopped
- Half mug (50 gram) chopped scallions
- two mugs (300 gram) chopped green bell pepper
- one mug (160 gram) chopped onion
- One-fourth tsp. garlic grains
- one tsp. Tabasco sauce

Instructions:

- Warm-up oven to 350-degree Fahrenheit. Merge ham, scallions, bell pepper, onion, and cheddar cheese.
- Put five tbsp. of batter on each tortilla and roll-up. Put seam side down in saucepan coated with nonstick margarine spray.
- In a separate pan, whisk together eggs and milk, flour, garlic, and Tabasco.
- Add over enchiladas. Put in freezer overnight.
- Enclose with foil and prepare for half an hour, uncovering for the last five minutes.

Delicious Frittata

Preparation Time: 45 Minutes

Cooking Time: 20 Minutes

Servings: 3

Ingredients:

- two mugs (226 gram) thinly diced zucchini
- one mug (150 gram) red bell pepper,
- One-fourth mug (60 milliliters) olive oil
- two baking potatoes, peeled and thinly diced
- one mug (160 gram) thinly diced onion
- one mug (150 gram) green bell pepper,
- 12 eggs
- two tbsp. chopped fresh parsley

Instructions:

- Heat the oven to 450-degree Fahrenheit. Add oil into a 12-inch (30-centimeter) sq. or spherical baking plate.
- Warm-up oil in the oven for 15 minutes, then take away. Put potatoes and onion over the bottom of the plate and prepare till potatoes are simply tender, 15 minutes.

- Arrange zucchini slices over potatoes and onion, then drizzle peppers over all. Whisk eggs.
- Add chopped parsley to eggs.
- Add eggs over vegetables. Prepare till eggs are set, and sides are "puffy," concerning 15 minutes. Beat ought to be golden toast.
- Serve hot or at area temperature.

Paleo Pasta Frittata

Preparation Time: 45 Minutes

Cooking Time: 15 Minutes

Servings: 4

Ingredients:

- one mug (160 gram) onion, chopped
- two mugs (100 gram) cooked pasta
- two tbsp. (30 milliliters) olive oil
- one mug (150 gram) red bell pepper, diced
- One-fourth mug (25 gram) minced Parmesan
- four eggs

Instructions:

- Warm-up a ten-in. (25-centimeter) a nonstick dish that's broiler safe. When the saucepan is hot, add the oil, then fry red bell pepper and onion for two to three minutes, moving frequently. Add the pasta to the saucepan, mixing well. When ingredients are combined, press down on pasta with a spatula to flatten it against the underside of the saucepan. Let it prepare a couple of minutes additional. Whisk minced Parmesan into the eggs.

- Add egg batter over the high of the pasta, creating sure the eggs spread evenly. Gently lift the sides of the pasta to let the egg flow beneath and completely coat the pasta. Let the eggs prepare for six to nine minutes. Slide the saucepan into a preheated broiler and end, making ready till eggs are set.

Healthy Strawberry Smoothie

Preparation Time: 10 Minutes

Cooking Time: 0 Minutes

Servings: 2

Ingredients:

- one tbsp. (13 gram) sugar
- one tsp. (five milliliters) lemon juice
- One-fourth of mugs (140 gram) strawberries
- one-Half mugs (355 milliliters) rice milk

Instructions:

- Put all ingredients in a blender and process until smooth. Serve immediately.

Paleo Oat Bran Waffles

Preparation Time: 50 Minutes

Cooking Time: 20 Minutes

Servings: 4

Ingredients:

- one egg
- third-fourth mug (180 milliliters) rice milk
- one tbsp. (15 milliliters) honey
- Half mug (60 gram) flour
- Half mug (40 gram) quick-preparing oats
- Half mug (50 gram) oat bran
- one tsp. baking grains
- two tbsp. (28 gram) without salt butter, melted

Instructions:

- Merge the first four ingredients. Mix egg, milk, honey, and butter. Add to dry ingredients, mixing until just blended.
- Prepare according to waffle iron mentioned instructions. Serve immediately.

Delicious Sundried Tomato Crackers

Preparation Time: 55 Minutes

Cooking Time: 15 Minutes

Servings: 3

Ingredients:

- One-fourth tsp. table salt or common salt
- one pinch of baking grains
- two dry-packed dried tomato halves
- three tbsp. (45 milliliters) boiling water
- one mug (145 gram) sunflower seeds
- Salt for sprinkling

Instructions:

- Fill a small plate halfway with boiling water and add your dried tomato halves.
- Allow them to soak for about 15 minutes or before they soften. Prepare your crackers as directed in the Simple Sunflower Crackers recipe, but add the rehydrated tomatoes and soaking water.
- Pulse the ingredients in the processor until they're evenly distributed in the dough.

- As for the rest of the sunflower crackers, roll them out and bake them.

Nutritional Analysis:

Calories: 224, Fat:11g, Carbohydrates: 13g, Sodium: 10mg, Protein: 1g, Net carbs: 2g

Couscous Cereal with Fruit

Preparation Time: 40 Minutes

Cooking Time: 15 Minutes

Servings: 4

Ingredients:

- third-fourth mug (180 milliliters) water
- Half mug (88 gram) couscous
- two tbsp. (20 gram) raisins
- two tbsp. (19 gram) dried cranberries
- one tbsp. (15 milliliters) honey
- Half tsp. cinnamon

Instructions:

- Carry water to a boil. Add the couscous and mix, then cover and remove from heat. Let stand for 15 minutes. Blend in the left-over ingredients.

Chicken and Guacamole Fry Egg

Preparation Time: 30 Minutes

Cooking Time: 15 Minutes

Servings: 2

Ingredients:

- two tbsp. (26 gram) coconut oil, or fat of choice
- one avocado
- two tbsp. (20 gram) chopped red onion
- , one garlic clove, or half a big one, crushed
- two tsp. lime juice
- Salt
- two oz. (55 gram) cooked chicken
- One-fourth mug (four-gram) chopped fresh cilantro, divided
- four eggs
- two pinches ground cumin
- two pinches oregano

Instructions:

- Chop your avocado in half and take away the seed by whacking it with the blade of a sharp knife and twisting. Use a spoon to scoop the avocado into a pan.

- Add the onion, the garlic, and the lime juice, and mash it up with a fork, leaving some texture.

- Style and judge if you wish table salt or common salt—I added very little. Now dice your chicken—you could use leftover turkey, for that matter.

- Chop the cilantro, too. Create your omelet consistent with Egg Fry Egg, adding the fat initially. Add a pinch of cumin and oregano to each pair of eggs as you whisk them. When your eggs are prepared for the filling, put in the chicken 1st, then spoon/spread guac on top.

- Drizzle in a very tbsp. (one gram) of cilantro and cover until done to taste. Transfer, plate, prime with another tbsp. (one gram) of cilantro, and cover to keep the heat while you create the second omelet.

Chocolate-Raspberry Smoothie

Preparation Time: 10 Minutes

Cooking Time: 0 Minutes

Servings: 2

Ingredients:

- one mug (235 milliliters) of rice milk
- Half mug (141 gram) chocolate syrup
- three mugs (750 gram) frozen raspberries

Instructions:

- Add the milk and chocolate syrup into a blender.
- Slowly add the raspberries, one mug at a time, and blend for 15 to 30 seconds after adding each mug.
- Do not overmix, as this will thin the drink down.
- Serve immediately.

Delicious Bacon-and-Egg Salad

Preparation Time: 20 Minutes

Cooking Time: 0 Minutes

Servings: 4

Ingredients:

- four slices cooked bacon, crumbled
- six eggs, hard-boiled, peeled and chopped
- one tomato, diced
- four scallions, diced
- four tbsp. (56 gram) Mayonnaise in the Jar

Instructions:

- Just blend everything and mix well.
- You can serve right away this with lettuce leaves to wrap it in, or be revolutionary and eat it with a fork.
- Serve immediately.

Coleslaw with Chicken, Strawberries, and Almonds

Preparation Time: 20 Minutes

Cooking Time: 0 Minutes

Servings: 3

Ingredients:

- eight mugs (560 gram) ground cabbage
- eight scallions
- one batch Poppy Seed Dressing
- Half mug (55 gram) slivered almonds
- eight big strawberries
- 12 oz. (340 gram) diced cooked chicken

Instructions:

- We're going to assume your dressing is already made, but if it's not, be sure of that initial.
- Put your almonds in a very dry dish and mix them over moderate-small heat until they're gently gold.
- Don't walk away! Just stand there and mix them, or those almonds can as soon burn as observe you.

- Cut your cabbage and throw it in a massive saucepan. Dice your scallions thin, together with the crisp half of the green shoot, and increase the saucepan. Dice your strawberries and add them to the pan.
- Now dice your chicken—I simply snip it right into the saucepan with my kitchen shears. Add on the dressing and toss to coat. Pile your salad on four plates, drizzle the almonds on high, and serve right away.

Low-Fat Mushroom and Pepper Quiche

Preparation Time: 35 Minutes

Cooking Time: 15 Minutes

Servings: 4

Ingredients:

- two tsp. (ten milliliters) olive oil
- one mug (160 gram) onion, chopped
- third-fourth mug (113 gram) green bell pepper, chopped
- two mugs (140 gram) mushroom, diced
- two cloves' garlic, chopped
- two lb. (900 gram) tofu
- Sliced tomatoes for garnish

Instructions:

- Warm-up oil in a moderate-sized dish. Fry vegetables and garlic until soft. In a big pan, crumble, or mash tofu. Add fried vegetables.
- Warm-up oven to 350-degree Fahrenheit. Layout tofu batters evenly into a quiche saucepan. Prepare one hour until the edges of the tofu start to toast. Garnish with tomatoes.

Delightful Vegetarian Vegetable Soup

Preparation Time: 45 Minutes

Cooking Time: 15 Minutes

Servings: 3

Ingredients:

- two mugs (360 gram) chopped tomato
- three potatoes, peeled and diced
- two turnips, peeled and diced
- three carrots, peeled and diced
- Half mug (50 gram) diced celery
- six mugs water
- one onion, chopped
- one tsp. black pepper
- one tsp. table salt or common salt-free seasoning
- one tsp. basil
- 12 oz. (340 gram) frozen mixed vegetables
- two mugs (140 gram) ground cabbage

Instructions:

- Put all ingredients in a big pot. Cook until vegetables are done.
- Serve immediately.

Low-Fat Apple and Barley Stew

Preparation Time: 60 Minutes

Cooking Time: 20 Minutes

Servings: 4

Ingredients:

- one mug (130 gram) carrot, diced
- one tsp. thyme
- One-fourth tsp. dried marjoram
- one bay leaf
- two mugs (250 gram) apples, unpeeled, chopped
- two mugs (320 gram) onion, thinly diced
- two tbsp. (30 milliliters) olive oil
- 3Half mug (825 milliliters) small- vegetable broth
- one-Half mugs (355 milliliters) apple cider
- one-third mug (67 gram) pearl barley
- One-fourth mug (15 gram) fresh parsley, chopped
- one tbsp. (15 milliliters) lemon juice

Instructions:

- In a small soup pot, fry onions in oil over moderate heat for 15 minutes, moving constantly.
- Decrease heat, cover, and prepare, frequently moving for five minutes more until onions are toasted.
- Add stock, cider, barley, carrots, thyme, marjoram, and bay leaf.
- Enclose and prepare for one hour or until barley is tender.
- Add apples, parsley, and lemon juice. Prepare for 15 minutes or until apples are slightly soft.
- Separate bay leaf and serve right away.

Delightful Baked Fried Potatoes

Preparation Time: 55 Minutes

Cooking Time: 25 Minutes

Servings: 3

Ingredients:

- four big potatoes
- one tbsp. (15 milliliters) olive oil

Instructions:

- Warm-up oven to 400-degree Fahrenheit. Scrub potatoes. Chop each in half lengthwise. Chop each half into four spears. Put potatoes in a big pot of boiling water, bring water back to a boil, and boil for three minutes.
- The shift in a colander. Cover a preparing sheet with nonstick margarine spray. Merge the olive oil and potatoes in a pan and toss to coat. Prepare for 15 minutes or until tender. Shift on paper towels.

Paleo Mashed Potatoes

Preparation Time: 30 Minutes

Cooking Time: 10 Minutes

Servings: 3

Ingredients:

- four moderate red potatoes
- Half tsp. roasted garlic
- two tbsp. (30 gram) fat-free cream cheddar cheese
- One-fourth mug (60 milliliters) rice milk
- one tsp. (one gram) chives
- one tbsp. (four-gram) fresh parsley, chopped.

Instructions:

- Dice the potatoes (you may peel them or leave them unpeeled). Put in a saucepan of water, bring to a boil, and boil until potatoes are soft but not mushy. Shift very well. Put potatoes in a big saucepan; add garlic, cream cheddar cheese, and milk.
- Whisk batter until it reaches desired consistency, adding more milk if needed, then add the chives and parsley and blend well.

Delicious Curried Chicken and Apples

Preparation Time: 25 Minutes

Cooking Time: 10 Minutes

Servings: 2

Ingredients:

- two boneless skinless chicken breasts
- , two tbsp. (42 gram) honey,
- two tsp. (four-gram) curry grains
- two apples, peeled and chopped
- three tbsp. oil
- Half mug (50 gram) celery, diced
- One-fourth mug (35 gram) raisins
- three tbsp. (one-two gram) fresh parsley

Instructions:

- Place the chicken in a pan and cut it into cubes. Combine the honey and curry powder with the chicken and mix well. Toss in the apples.
- Warm the oil in a heavy-bottomed pan over high pressure. One minute of celery frying three-four minutes, or before the chicken is no longer pink, add apple batter and mix-fry. Mix in the raisins and parsley, then serve right away over rice.

Delicious Cheese Pie

Preparation Time: 55 Minutes

Cooking Time: 20 Minutes

Servings: 2

Ingredients:

- third-fourth mug (180 milliliters) rice milk
- One-fourth tsp. black pepper
- four oz. (115 gram) feta cheddar cheese
- 16 oz. (455 gram) small fat ricotta cheddar cheese
- four eggs
- One-fourth mug (30 gram) flour

Instructions:

- Warm-up oven to 375-degree Fahrenheit. Sprinkle an ovenproof dish or glass baking plate with non-stick margarine spray.
- Merge the cheeses, then mix in the eggs, flour, milk, and pepper. Add the batter into the prepared saucepan. Prepare for 40 minutes, or until golden and set. Chop into wedges.

Spaghetti with Mexican Vegetables

Preparation Time: 35 Minutes

Cooking Time: 10 Minutes

Servings: 2

Ingredients:

- Half tsp. chopped garlic
- one tsp. Mexican seasoning
- Half mug (120 milliliters) dry white wine
- 30 cherry tomatoes, halved
- 12 oz. (340 gram) spaghetti
- two tbsp. (30 milliliters) olive oil
- one mug (150 gram) red bell pepper, chopped in strips
- one mug (150 gram) yellow bell pepper, chopped in strips
- one mug (160 gram) onion, thinly diced
- One-fourth mug (20 gram) Parmesan, ground

Instructions:

- Prepare spaghetti as directed on the box. Shift the water.
- Warm the oil in a large dish or the oven.
- Fry the peppers and onion until softened, then add the garlic, Mexican seasoning, and wine and continue to cook for a few minutes more, moving the pan to clear any stuck-on ingredients.
- Add the tomatoes and cook until they soften slightly.
- Add the spaghetti and mix well. Cheddar cheese is added to the mix.

Turkey Carcass Soup

Preparation Time: 55 Minutes

Cooking Time: 20 Minutes

Servings: 3

Ingredients:

- four mugs (950 milliliters), chicken broth
- one mug (235 milliliters) of dry red wine
- one-Half mugs (195 gram) chopped carrot
- two mugs (300 gram) chopped turnip
- Half mug (97 gram) rice
- one turkey carcass, most meats removed
- three quarts water
- one tbsp. peppercorns
- one mug (100 gram) chopped celery
- two mugs (320 gram) chopped onion
- Half mug (100 gram) pearl barley

Instructions:

- In a big pot, barely cover turkey carcass with water. Add peppercorns and half of the chopped onion and celery.

- Cook for 40 minutes. Shift, save the liquid and pick left-over meat from the carcass.
- In saved liquid, add meat, chicken broth, and red wine; boil for half an hour.
- Add the rest of the ingredients.
- Cook until rice and barley are tender, at least 40 minutes, and two hours or more.

Savory Beef Stew

Preparation Time: 55 Minutes

Cooking Time: 25 Minutes

Servings: 2

Ingredients:

- two mugs (360 gram) canned no-table salt or common salt-added tomatoes
- Half mug (120 milliliters) water
- two tbsp. (30 gram) toast sugar
- one tbsp. (15 milliliters) Worcestershire sauce
- two tbsp. (16 gram) flour
- one lb. (455 gram) beef round steak, diced
- two tbsp. (30 milliliters) olive oil
- four moderate potatoes, diced
- one mug (130 gram) carrot, diced
- Half mug (80 gram) onion, coarsely chopped
- one mug (235 milliliters) small beef broth
- Half tsp. ground ginger
- One-fourth tsp. ground allspice

Instructions:

- Fill a plastic bag of flour. Shake to powder the beef. Warm the oil in a large dish over medium heat.
- Both sides of the beef should be toasted. In a slow cooker, combine the potatoes, carrots, and onion. Beef is used to beat.
- Combine the remaining ingredients and pour over the meat and vegetables.
- Enclose and cook for eight to ten hours on low or four to five hours on average.

Delightful Greek Fish Stew

Preparation Time: 60 Minutes

Cooking Time: 20 Minutes

Servings: 3

Ingredients:

- one tsp. (two gram) fennel seed
- two mugs (360 gram) canned no-table salt or common salt-added tomatoes
- two mugs (470 gram) small chicken broth
- one tbsp. dried parsley
- Half tsp. (one gram) black pepper
- One-fourth tsp. turmeric
- four oz. (115 gram) orzo, or other small pasta
- Half mug (80 gram) onion, chopped
- Half tsp. chopped garlic

Instructions:

- Prepare pasta according to package directions. Shift and set aside.
- In a big non-stick saucepan coated with non-stick margarine spray, prepare onions, garlic, and fennel seed until onion is tender.

- Add tomatoes, broth, parsley, pepper, and turmeric. Decrease heat and boil for five minutes.
- Add fish and boil for five minutes, or until fish is cooked through.
- Divide pasta among four bowls. Ladle soup over pasta.

Swedish Salmon Stew

Preparation Time: 55 Minutes

Cooking Time: 20 Minutes

Servings: 3

Ingredients:

- Half mug (120 milliliters) white wine
- One-fourth mug (60 milliliters) sherry
- Half mug (115 gram) fat-free sour cream
- one-Half lb. (680 gram) potatoes, peeled and diced
- one-Half lb. (680 gram) salmon fillets
- one tbsp. (four-gram) fresh dill, chopped
- One-fourth mug (60 milliliters) olive oil, heated

Instructions:

- Warm-up oven to 350-degree Fahrenheit. Cook potatoes for ten to 15 minutes, or until almost done. Layer potato slices in a big ovenproof casserole.
- Put the salmon on top. Drizzle with the dill and drizzle with the olive oil. Enclose and prepare for 15 minutes. Separate from the oven and add the wine and sherry over.

Low-Fat Dilly Tuna Salad

Preparation Time: 30 Minutes

Cooking Time: 15 Minutes

Servings: 2

Ingredients:

- three tbsp. (12 gram) fresh dill chopped
- two tbsp. (20 gram) white onions, diced
- one mug (284 gram) light tuna, in water, drained
- One-fourth mug (25 gram) celery, chopped
- two tbsp. (28 gram) small-fat mayonnaise
- Pepper to taste

Instructions:

- Merge all ingredients well. Serve immediately with mint sauce.

Barbecued Fish

Preparation Time: 60 Minutes

Cooking Time: 25 Minutes

Servings: 3

Ingredients:

- one tbsp. (15 milliliters) Worcestershire sauce
- two tsp. (ten-gram) instant chopped onion
- one lb. (455 gram) catfish
- One-fourth mug (60 milliliters) small- catsup

Instructions:

- Put fish fillets in a not-greased baking saucepan. Merge catsup, lemon juice, Worcestershire sauce, sugar, onion, and pepper sauce.
- Add on fish; turn until both sides are coated. Enclose and freeze for half an hour. Warm-up oven to 400-degree Fahrenheit. Prepare, uncovered, until fish flakes easily with a fork, 15 to 30 minutes.

Spicy Grilled Chicken with Green Onions

Preparation Time: 60 Minutes

Cooking Time: 25 Minutes

Servings: 3

Ingredients:

- two tsp. Honey,
- one tsp. paprika
- two tbsp. (30 milliliters) margarine
- one tbsp. (15 milliliters) Tabasco sauce
- seven green onions
- two chicken breasts, boned and skinned

Instructions:

- Prepare the grill (moderate-high heat). Whisk oil, Tabasco, honey, and paprika in a nine-in. (twenty-three centimeter) glass pie plate to mix.
- Mince one green onion and mix it into the marinade.
- Transfer two tbsp. (thirty milliliters) of the marinade to a small pan and reserve.
- Add chicken to the pie plate marinade and flip to coat.

- Let stand five minutes, turning sometimes.
- Grill chicken and whole onions until chicken is cooked through and onions soften, occasionally turning about five minutes.
- Transfer chicken and grilled onions to plates and drizzle with one tbsp. (15 milliliters) each of the reserved marinade.

Low-Fat Fish Fritter

Preparation Time: 50 Minutes

Cooking Time: 20 Minutes

Servings: 4

Ingredients:

- One-eighth tsp. pepper
- One-eighth tsp. garlic grains
- one lb. (455 gram) cod
- three eggs, separated
- three tbsp. (24 gram) flour
- one tbsp. (four-gram) fresh parsley, chopped

Instructions:

- Prepare fish, remove skin and bones, and mash. Whisk egg yolks until light and thick; then add flour, pepper, garlic, parsley, and fish.
- Transfer in whites of eggs beaten until stiff. Drop by tbsp. Into hot deep fat and fry until golden toast.

Maryland Crab Soup

Preparation Time: 55 Minutes

Cooking Time: 20 Minutes

Servings: 3

Ingredients:

- Half mug (65 gram) no-table salt or common salt-added frozen peas
- one-Half tsp. seafood seasoning (Old Bay is traditional)
- Half tsp. black pepper
- one lb. (455 gram) crabmeat
- two mugs (475 milliliters) small- chicken broth
- two mugs (480 gram) diced no-table salt or common salt-added canned tomatoes
- Half mug (82 gram) frozen corn
- Half tsp. cayenne pepper

Instructions:

- Put all ingredients in a big saucepan and boil until the crabmeat and vegetables are cooked. Serve right away.

Chicken in Sour Cream Sauce

Preparation Time: 35 Minutes

Cooking Time: 15 Minutes

Servings: 3

Ingredients:

- Half tsp. rosemary
- two tbsp. (eight gram) fresh parsley
- Half tsp. thyme
- one tbsp. (nine gram) green pepper, finely chopped
- two lb. (900 gram) boneless skinless chicken breast
- Half mug (half a gram) without salt butter
- Half-pint (230 gram) fat-free sour cream
- Half mug (120 milliliters) sherry
- Pepper to taste
- Half mug (55 gram) slivered almonds

Instructions:

- Toast chicken in butter in the dish. Put in casserole.
- Add sour cream and sherry to chicken drippings.

- Add left-over ingredients and boil for five minutes.
- Add batter over chicken pieces. Prepare 350-degree Fahrenheit for one hour.
- Serve immediately.

Slow Cooker Chicken in Tomato Cream Sauce

Preparation Time: 60 Minutes

Cooking Time: 30 Minutes

Servings: 3

Ingredients:

- one mug (235 milliliters) fat-free evaporated milk
- two egg yolks
- third-fourth mug (75 gram) parmesan cheddar cheese, minced
- two chicken breasts halves
- two tbsp. {30 milliliters} olive oil
- One-fourth mug (25 gram) green onions, chopped
- one tsp. garlic, chopped
- 14 Half oz. (41 gram) canned tomatoes drained and chopped
- one tbsp. basil
- eight oz. (225 gram) fettuccine
- one mug (130 gram) frozen peas, thawed
- one-Half mug (one 05 gram) mushrooms, diced

Instructions:

- In a dish, toast chicken breasts in olive oil. Put chicken in the slow cooker. Add green onions, garlic, tomatoes, and basil. Enclose and prepare on Low seven to nine hours. Separate chicken and chop into pieces. Return chicken pieces to the pot.
- Blend in cream, egg yolks, and Parmesan cheddar cheese. Enclose and prepare on high for half an hour to thicken. While sauce is thickening, prepare fettuccine according to package directions; drain. Add fettuccine, peas, and mushrooms. Enclose and prepare on high 30 to one hour.

Delicious Vegetarian Lasagne

Preparation Time: 30 Minutes

Cooking Time: 15 Minutes

Servings: 3

Ingredients:

- 15 oz. (425 gram) ricotta cheddar cheese
- Half mug (40 gram) Parmesan, ground
- four oz. (115 gram) part-skim mozzarella, ground
- two tbsp. dried parsley
- two tbsp. (30 milliliters) olive oil
- one mug (160 gram) onion, chopped
- six mugs, small spaghetti sauce
- 12 oz. (340 gram) frozen spinach, thawed and drained
- two eggs
- 12 oz. (340 gram) lasagna noodles, cooked and drained

Instructions:

- Warm-up oven to 350-degree Fahrenheit.
- Heat olive oil in a very massive dish over moderate-high heat.
- Fry onion until lightly toasted.
- Add spaghetti sauce and mix to blend. In a huge pan, blend the spinach, ricotta, Parmesan, mozzarella, parsley, and eggs.

- Sprinkle a baking saucepan with non-stick margarine spray.
- Put a layer of tomato sauce in the bottom of the saucepan.
- Layer noodles, tomato sauce, and ricotta batter in that order, making three layers of every.
- Add a further layer of noodles and sauce on the high.
- Prepare, covered with foil, for sixty to 715 minutes, or until effervescent and heated through.
- Separate the foil and prepare ten minutes longer.

Low-Fat Grill Pork Chops

Preparation Time: 55 Minutes

Cooking Time: 15 Minutes

Servings: 3

Ingredients:

- Half tsp. dry mustard
- one tbsp. (15 milliliters) Worcestershire sauce
- one tsp. (two gram) black pepper
- pork loin chops, one inch thick
- one mug (160 gram) onion, finely chopped
- two tbsp. (30 milliliters) acetic acid
- one tbsp. (15 milliliters) canola oil
- one tbsp. (13 gram) sugar
- Half tsp. paprika

Instructions:

- Score the edges of the chops to prevent curling. Put into a big baking saucepan; set aside.
- Mix left-over ingredients and blend well.
- Add over the chops to coat well. Enclose and chill for two to four hours.
- Grill chops to desired doneness, basting often n.

Gluten-Free Pork Chop and Bean Skillet

Preparation Time: 55 Minutes

Cooking Time: 25 Minutes

Servings: 2

Ingredients:

- Half tsp. chopped garlic
- Half mug (120 milliliters) small chicken broth
- Half mug (125 gram) barbecue sauce
- six center-chop pork chops
- one tbsp. (15 milliliters) olive oil
- one mug (160 gram) chopped onion
- two jalapeño peppers, chopped
- four mugs (684 gram) no-table salt or common salt-added pinto beans, drained

Instructions:

- In a big dish, sear pork chops in oil until toast, about 15 minutes. Separate pork chops and put on plate. Add onion and garlic to dish; prepare five minutes. Blend in broth, barbecue sauce, jalapeños, and beans.

- Warm-up batter to a boil. Return pork to dish. Decrease heat. Enclose and boil 50 to one hour, moving sauce and turning chops infrequently until meat is fork-tender.

Amazing Apple and Pork Chop Skillet

Preparation Time: 60 Minutes

Cooking Time: 30 Minutes

Servings: 3

Ingredients:

- two tbsp. (13 gram) fresh ginger, peeled and thinly diced
- one apple, peeled and thinly diced
- Half mug (120 milliliters) water
- one tbsp. (15 milliliters) olive oil
- Half mug (80 gram) onion, chopped
- three pork loin chops

Instructions:

- Warm-up oil in a non-stick dish over moderate heat. Fry the chopped onion for two to four minutes, or until lightly toasted. Push the onion pieces to one side of the dish and put the chops in the center of the dish.
- Toast the chops on each side. Spoon the onion pieces on top of each chop, dividing evenly. Layer each chop with diced ginger and apple. Add the

water to the dish and cover tightly. Prepare over small heat for one hour depending on the thickness of the pork chops.

Delicious Asian Lasagne

Preparation Time: 60 Minutes

Cooking Time: 25 Minutes

Servings: 3

Ingredients:

- two mugs (460 gram) refried beans
- two third-fourth mugs (645 milliliters) no-table salt or common salt-added tomato sauce
- Half mug (115 gram) salsa
- Half mug (30 gram) chopped fresh cilantro, divided
- third-fourth lb. (340 gram) lasagna noodles
- Half mug (80 gram) onion, chopped
- Half mug (75 gram) red bell pepper, chopped
- Half mug (82 gram) frozen corn kernels, thawed
- Half tsp. chopped garlic
- two mugs (450 gram) canned black beans, rinsed and drained
- One-fourth mug (58 gram) fat-free sour cream
- One-fourth mug (50 gram) black olives, diced

Instructions:

- Heat-up oven to 350-degree Fahrenheit. Carry a massive pot of lightly salted water to a boil. Add pasta and prepare for eight to five minutes or until al dente. Shift. Cover a huge dish with non-stick margarine spray and place over moderate heat. Fry onion, red bell pepper, corn, and garlic until tender. Blend in black beans, refried beans, tomato sauce, salsa, and One-fourth mug (fifteen gram) cilantro.

- Prepare till heated through and slightly condensed; put aside. In a massive pan, mix cottage cheddar cheese, ricotta, sour cream, Monterey Jack cheddar cheese, and left-over One-fourth mug (15 gram) chopped cilantro; put aside.

- Cover a casserole plate with non-stick margarine spray. Arrange three of the cooked lasagna noodles in the underside of the plate, cutting to fit if necessary. Layout with one-third of the bean batter, then one-third of the cheddar cheese batter. Repeat layers twice additional. Enclose and prepare for 40 minutes. Garnish with diced black olives.

Asian Beef Soup

Preparation Time: 40 Minutes

Cooking Time: 20 Minutes

Servings: 3

Ingredients:

- one mug (240 gram) no-table salt or common salt-added canned tomatoes
- two mugs (500 gram) Asian-flavored beans
- Half lb. (225 gram) extra-lean ground beef, 93 percent lean
- Half mug (80 gram) chopped onion
- one mug (70 gram) ground cabbage
- one mug (235 milliliters) water

Instructions:

- Toast beef and onion in a big saucepan. Shift. Add cabbage and continue preparing until cabbage are soft, about 15 minutes. Add tomatoes, beans, and water. Carry to boil and boil five minutes to blend the flavors.

Asian Steak Salad

Preparation Time: 35 Minutes

Cooking Time: 15 Minutes

Servings: 4

Ingredients:

- One-fourth mug (25 gram) green onions, diced
- eight oz. (225 gram) beef round steak, cooked and diced (about two mugs)
- one small head iceberg lettuce, ground
- Half mug (115 gram) sour cream
- Half mug (130 gram) salsa
- two tbsp. (two gram) fresh cilantro, divided
- one mug (256 gram) kidney beans, rinsed and drained
- five radishes, thinly diced
- one avocado, peeled and diced
- 30 tortilla chips (about two oz.)

Instructions:

- In small pan, blend sour cream, salsa, and one tbsp. (one gram) cilantro; set aside. In moderate pan blend beans, cheddar cheese, green onions, and left-over one tbsp. (one gram) cilantro.
- To serve right away, on four individual plates arrange bean batter, beef, lettuce, radishes, avocado, olives, and tortilla chips. Serve with dressing.

Delicious Cranberry Pork Roast

Preparation Time: 50 Minutes

Cooking Time: 15 Minutes

Servings: 4

Ingredients:

- one tsp. orange peel, minced
- one-eighth tsp. cloves
- three lb. (one one-third kg) pork loin roast
- one mug (110 gram) cranberries, finely chopped
- One-fourth mug (85 gram) honey
- one-eighth tsp. nutmeg

Instructions:

- Put roast in slow cooker. Mix left-over ingredients. Add over roast. Enclose. Prepare on small for eight to ten hours. Serve right away.

Chili Chicken Breasts

Preparation Time: 30 Minutes

Cooking Time: 15 Minutes

Servings: 3

Ingredients:

- One-fourth tsp. garlic grains
- four boneless chicken breasts
- two tbsp. (30 milliliters) olive oil
- one-third mug (80 milliliters) lime juice
- two tbsp. (six milliliters) chopped green chilis
- four oz. (115 gram) small-fat Swiss cheddar cheese
- Salsa, for serving

Instructions:

- A nine-inch (23-centimeter) square baking saucepan combines the olive oil, lime juice, chilis, and garlic grains. Add chicken breasts; marinate in the freezer for at least 40 minutes, turning once. Separate chicken from marinade; drain.
- Grill or fry chicken for seven minutes; flip over and continue making ready for six to eight

minutes, or until done. Beat each chicken breast with a slice of cheddar cheese. Continue preparing till cheddar cheese begins to melt. Serve with salsa.

Low-Fat Poached Salmon

Preparation Time: 45 Minutes

Cooking Time: 25 Minutes

Servings: 3

Ingredients:

- Half mug (80 gram) onion, thinly diced
- one bay leaf
- four mugs (946 milliliters) water
- two tbsp. (30 milliliters) lemon juice
- One-fourth mug (30 gram) carrot, thinly diced
- one tbsp. (four gram) fresh dill, chopped
- Half lb. (225 gram) salmon fillets

Instructions:

- Warm-up oven to 350-degree Fahrenheit. Mix all ingredients except salmon in a saucepan and heat to boiling. Decrease heat and boil 15 minutes.
- Put salmon in a glass baking plate big enough to hold salmon in a single layer; add poaching liquid over. Enclose and prepare for 15 minutes, or until salmon flakes easily.

Delicious Chicken and Mushroom Quesadillas

Preparation Time: 40 Minutes

Cooking Time: 15 Minutes

Servings: 3

Ingredients:

- eight oz. (225 gram) mushrooms, diced
- one mug (110 gram) chicken breast, cooked and ground
- two-third mug (110 gram) onion, finely chopped
- Half mug (30 gram) fresh cilantro, chopped
- one tbsp. (15 milliliters) olive oil
- two Half tsp. chili grains
- Half tsp. chopped garlic
- one tsp. (one gram) dried oregano
- 16 five Half-inch (13.75-centimeter) corn tortillas

Instructions:

- Warm-up olive oil during a big dish over moderate-high heat. Add chili grains, garlic, and oregano and fry for one minute. Add mushrooms and fry for five minutes, or until tender. Separate from heat and mix in the chicken, onion, and cilantro. Chill for five minutes, then mix within the cheddar cheese.

- Sprinkle olive oil spray on one aspect of eight of the tortillas and place them oiled-facet down on a baking sheet. Divide chicken batter among tortillas, spreading to a good thickness. Beat with the left-over tortillas and spray the tops with olive oil spray. Grill quesadillas for three minutes per aspect, or until heated through and golden toast. Chop into wedges to serve instantly.

Amazing Banana Bites

Preparation Time: 30 Minutes

Cooking Time: 0 Minutes

Servings: 2

Ingredients:

- six oz. (213 gram) orange juice concentrate
- three mugs (450 gram) diced banana
- two mugs (164 gram) granola

Instructions:

- Chop bananas into bite-size pieces. Add orange juice concentrate into mixing pan. Layout granola on baking sheet. Dip banana bits into the orange juice. Roll in granola.

Crave Special Greek Chicken Drumettes

Preparation Time: 40 Minutes

Cooking Time: 15 Minutes

Servings: 3

Ingredients:

- two chicken wings
- three tbsp. (45 milliliters) lemon juice
- two tbsp. (30 milliliters) olive oil
- two tbsp. (40 gram) honey
- one tsp. oregano
- one garlic clove, chopped

Instructions:

- Separate chicken wings into sections. Separate wing tips. Mix all ingredients except chicken in a big resealable plastic bag. Merge well. Add chicken, seal, and turn to coat. Freeze eight hours or overnight. Separate chicken from marinade and put in baking saucepan. Prepare at 400-degree Fahrenheit for one hour until golden toast.

Delicious Tortilla Roll-Ups

Preparation Time: 45 Minutes

Cooking Time: 20 Minutes

Servings: 3

Ingredients:

- eight oz. (225 gram) cream cheddar cheese
- four oz. (115 gram) black olives, chopped
- four oz. (115 gram) diced green chilis
- One-fourth tsp. Tabasco sauce
- eight whole wheat tortillas

Instructions:

- Cream together cream cheddar cheese, olives, chilis, and Tabasco sauce. Layout approximately two tbsp. onto a tortilla, roll jelly-roll fashion, roll in plastic wrap, and chill. Before serving, unwrap and chop into two-centimeter-wide pieces.

Fat-Free Potato Chips

Preparation Time: 40 Minutes

Cooking Time: 15 Minutes

Servings: 3

Ingredients:

- four moderate potatoes
- Your choice of spices or herbs

Instructions:

- If the potatoes are old, peel them before slicing. If the potatoes are new or have good skins, do not peel, just scrub well.
- Dice potatoes one/16 inch (one. Five mm) in thickness, slicing across the potato.
- Drizzle with your choice of spices or herbs, if you want.
- If you have a microwave bacon tray, put the diced potatoes flat on the tray in a single layer.
- Enclose with a microwavable, round, heavy plastic cover.
- If you do not have a bacon tray, put potatoes between two microwave-safe plates.

- Microwave on high (full power) for seven to eight minutes.
- Cooking time could vary slightly, depending on the wattage of your microwave. You do not have to turn the diced potatoes over.
- Plates will be hot by the time potatoes are done.
- Continue to microwave the remainder of diced potatoes as directed above.

Marinated Veggies

Preparation Time: 50 Minutes

Cooking Time: 20 Minutes

Servings: 2

Ingredients:

- Half mug (35 gram) chopped mushrooms
- One-fourth mug (25 gram) chopped black olives
- One-fourth mug (25 gram) chopped green olives
- Half mug (82 gram) cooked chickpeas
- Half tsp. chopped garlic
- Half mug (120 milliliters) acetic acid
- Half mug (120 milliliters) olive oil
- one tsp. oregano
- Half mug (80 gram) chopped onion
- Half mug (150 gram) chopped artichoke hearts

Instructions:

- Mix first four ingredients. Add any or all of the left-over ingredients, cut raw vegetables into bite-size chunks, and drain liquids from those in cans. Marinate up to 24 hours.

Amazing Chocolate Peanut Cookies

Preparation Time: 60 Minutes

Cooking Time: 20 Minutes

Servings: 3

Ingredients:

- 45-gram chocolate candy bar
- four tbsp. (64 gram) crunchy peanut butter
- one mug (60 gram) lightly sweetened bran cereal,

Instructions:

- Microwave the chocolate bar and peanut butter until smooth, about 30 seconds at a time. Take caution not to overheat. To combine the melted chocolate and peanut butter, use a blender. Toss in the cereal and softly toss until evenly covered.
- Prepare six cookies by dropping them on waxed paper or foil. Freeze for 30 minutes, then place in resealable plastic bags and store in the refrigerator.

Nutritional Analysis:

Calories: 219, Fat:17g, Carbohydrates: 21g, Sodium: 11mg, Protein: 2g, Net carbs: 1g

NOTE